Home Business No More 9 to 5!

Be Your Own Boss, Work from Home, and Make Money Online

By

ALAN ANDERSON

Alan Anderson

Alan Anderson

are expressed or implied. Readers acknowledge that the author is not engaging in the rendering of legal, financial, medical, or professional advice.

Table of Contents

Chapter 5: The Best Online Business Model for You 31

Introduction

Right about now, you should know something that is very important. You will see it here, and I will mention it a few times throughout the book and then again at the end. In a word, it is called commitment. You have to be committed to quitting the rat race, or it will never happen. You can think it, and you can wish for it, but not until you commit to it will it become a reality. So how do you commit to it? Very simply... again, in one word: ACTION. You must take action, and everything will fall into place. You will create an outline with your game plan by writing it down, you will attach a timeframe to it, you will put it down on paper by your night stand, you will read it before going to bed, you will read it when you wake up, and you will take ACTION to make it happen.

The only thing necessary to make all this happen costs nothing, nada, zilch. That "thing" is "belief," as in believe in yourself. If you believe that you can do it, you can. So to sum it all up: Believe–Commit–Act.

Alan Anderson

Chapter 1: Jumpstarting a Home Business

Working from home is not as simple as quitting your job, making an office out of your bedroom, and then starting to sell products or offer services around your town. Financial freedom does not come that easily because a home business has more sacrifices than rewards at first. You have to wait for it to peak before you can truly say that you are indeed a home businessman who no longer needs regular paychecks and paid leaves to enjoy life and attain financial security.

The idea of owning a business straight from the comforts of your home at your own time is really exciting. However, the journey towards achieving actual success will definitely be time-consuming, stressful, and at times, frustrating.

As you read this chapter, start writing down your ideas and plans according to these guides towards jumpstarting your biggest avenue to work from home, and you actually earn from it.

Choose a product or service

What do you want to do: sell a product or offer a service? If you will sell a product, what kind of product will it be? Are you planning to make one on your own, like homemade soaps, or sell retail items, like antiques or collectibles? Selling products will also include possible problems on storage, delivery, ordering, manufacturing, packaging, and retailing. Needless to say, selling tangible products can entail bigger capital, as there are more facilities, personnel, and volume required before the business can actually start its operation.

If you want to offer a service, do you even have the skills or technical expertise to back it up? With this type of business, your biggest investment will be your own time and skills, so lacking in that department will definitely not help you gain reputation and credibility in your target market. Moreover, consider the extra manpower that is commonly needed for a service-type business, plus the equipment – usually industrial levels – that might be necessary.

As much as possible, choose something that you really have knowledge on or something that you really love. Excitement wears off after stress and frustration set in, but passion will always be there, regardless of the hardships that you will face in running a home business.

Lastly, as early as in the conceptualizing and planning stages, check possible suppliers, distributors, and partners, preferably near your area, just to make sure that everything is really practical for you. It might surprise you, but working from home does not entail exclusively working from home. There are raw materials and finished products that will come in and out of your house. There will be clients that you have to meet outside or entertain right at the comforts of your workstation. There might even be stores involved, like in the case of makeshift shops and in-house stores, literally.

Set your mission and vision

What exactly do you want to achieve with starting a home business? Is it financial freedom? You surely can go even more specific, like a certain level of income, future investment like a new house or car, longevity in the business, expansion to different states, and cracking the Fortune 500. Google and Amazon both started as home businesses, but look at where they are now.

Your vision will be your beacon when things get rough and the road ahead already seems dark or seems like a dead end. It will bring you back to your core, which is very important because a home business simply starts with a dream, with a lot of risks to your professional growth and personal life.

Meanwhile, your mission will keep you on track and looking forward to a specific action that you want to do.

From the point of view of customers, a mission and vision are commitments to doing right and offering high quality. They show the public that you are aiming at a positive direction and that you are doing something not out of a whim.

Size the competition, size the market

This is where feasibility study and market research come in. You need factual data and statistics to back up your plan, most especially if you will approach banks and private investors for your startup capital. You cannot be successful in a business if you do not have a market for it, that is, people who have money and are willing to spend them.

Conducting research about the competition will help you achieve improved products and services, marketing strategy, business structure, and customer relations management. It will also show you your exact position in the industry within your specific market or location, which is important to identify fields of improvement and development. You also do not want to go over the standard pricing and quality that customers prefer from your potential competitors.

Starting a business that has no competitor is nice because you have a whole market to yourself. However, be aware of the dangers because lack of competition breeds substandard quality. For practical reasons, it is also necessary to check thoroughly why a certain business has not been set up in your place or elsewhere as well. It is either you are a business genius who has thought of a brilliant idea that no other businessman has ever thought of before, or other businessmen are just not dumb enough to invest in a suicidal venture.

As much as possible, study the systems and strategies of your competitors. Adapt what is a success, and throw out what is a failure. Learn from other businessmen's mistakes.

Double check your location

Your home might be conducive for living, but is it also marketable? Look at your population, foot traffic, culture, employment rate, salary level, and social class. This is still classified as a home business, practically and legally.

Location is not a problem if your business will be entirely online. However, do understand that you might still need to receive, store, and distribute supplies, which all require space. Is your house built for that?

Register your business

Working from home is still working, wherever you stay, so you need a tax identification number unless you want the IRA knocking on your door. That means you have to make things legal, whether you are employed or freelancing. If there will be an actual commercial transaction happening, like when selling products or offering services, you have to be registered to become legal. This covers the registration of your business name and brand and getting the trademark for your logo, tagline, and product/service.

Procuring a business license is also required, but additional licenses might be necessary depending on the type of business you have. For instance, a business falling under the health and food industries will need additional Environment, Health, and Safety (EHS) and sanitary permits prior to operation. Some states also require documentary approvals from the Health Department and Occupational Safety and Health Organization (OSHA).

Fortunately, some states no longer require permits after registration has been done. A home and small business may even operate without a business permit in certain cities.

Finally, your legal structure should also be thought about because this will affect your government support, loan capacity, tax amount, and allowable number of personnel.

Check if your small home business venture is more appropriate for a sole proprietorship, partnership (probably with your spouse or parents), company, LLC, or corporation. A small business normally falls under company.

Check special requirements from the Department of Consumers and Regulatory Affairs (state-dependent), Office of Zoning (for any form of land cultivation and development for commercial purposes), Department of Health (for anything that concerns public health and safety, like with a catering business), and the Department of Transportation (for public space regulation).

Hire and train

A mom-and-pop normally does not need additional hiring because all the family members help out with the business. However, if you will need extra hands from outside, like for production, servicing, delivery, selling, etc., you certainly need to learn the intricate system of hiring. There are seminars given by local governments for home and startup businessmen to assist them in the hiring and training process. Usually, the United States Small Business Administration (SBA) also provides free training.

Identify areas where you will need extra hands, so you do not have to over-hire.

Chapter 2: Creating Your Online Marketing Plan

An online business is now synonymous to home business simply because almost all marketing and selling efforts are concentrated on the internet as its primary – and on many cases, only – platform. The internet is the simplest, cheapest, and most convenient way to launch your own business to the world without the limitations that traditional business structure and operation commonly have. Creating your business' online marketing plan is not as easy as setting up a blog and paying for pay-per-click advertisements (PPC). You have to carefully plan it, as what is made online cannot be easily undone.

The internet is the most effective platform for marketing because of its wide network that allows information to spread like a wildfire, reaching millions of target consumers in just a matter of hours. However, as powerful as it is, the internet can also be a poison that can easily creep into your system, destroying your reputation across regions because what is released to the internet stays there with infinite duration.

Needless to say, you have to be very careful about conceptualizing and executing your marketing plan online because this will dictate half of your home business' direction – whether it will go up or down. Do not waste your opportunity to capture a portion of the market and establish a reputable name of your own. Follow these nine golden tips in creating your online marketing plan.

Join online forums and social media discussions

Online forums are excellent venues to disseminate information and create awareness about your brand because people are participating and interacting and are curious about what other people have to say. It is free, and the best part of it is that you can start conversations concentrated only on your specific field, in your specific location, about your specific business. Some businesses even use forum sites for the reviews of their products and services.

For many consumers, forums are more credible than review sites because there, it is just ordinary people with ordinary experience who are talking – no complications, no technicalities – just pure honest opinions. Apparently, it is a great way to reach down to your target market, appealing to them at a personal level rather than from a professional standpoint.

Gathering customer feedback through forums is also more practical as the comments are more natural, straight-to-the-point, and uninfluenced. At the same time, you can immediately answer their concerns for other people to see, simply to let them know that you are taking action based on what they have to say. Moreover, forums are great venues to drop your backlinks without looking desperate for traffic.

Just keep in mind: no spamming and hostile reasoning.

Spend on your website design

Website design is the first thing visitors notice when they enter a site. Whether it is a blog or Facebook page, you have to make your main site attractive to keep customers coming in and new visitors hooked. If you are not adept in the graphic design department, better let the professionals handle it. Remember that your website design is a long-term investment, same as how receptions, lobbies, and building facades greet clients in real business offices.

Compare the well-designed websites of Fortune 500 companies to the scam-laden websites of multi-level marketing companies. Are they different in terms of structure, navigation, design, and content? Legitimate business websites tend to be clean, comprehensive, navigable, and simple, while unprofessional-looking ones are cluttered, filled with startling effects and screaming headlines, lack internal navigation and linking, non-user friendly, and in some cases, riddled with malware and spyware.

A good business website design should be engaging but not overly designed, because over-designing means desperation. Focus your graphic design on your banner and sales page to make your products and services more appealing to customers. Internal navigation and linking should not be "dead" to allow your visitors to go back and forth through pages without getting lost. The sales page should be user-friendly, with features such as *add to cart, order now, view details,* and a lot more security features.

Furthermore, all your business information, professional background, product and service details, mission and vision, and all the mechanics on how to use the website and do transactions should be clearly presented. If you need articles and presentations but simply do not have the acumen to transform your ingenuity to words, hire a freelance writer. There are a lot of freelancing sites where you can pull your manpower from, such as Elance, Thumbtack, Freelancer, and ODesk. Craigslist is also popular but has more scammers than the rest.

In your overall design, do not forget to utilize one-click buttons that provide convenience to customers. A readily available one-click button is also sometimes the last push customers need to spend. These buttons include order buttons and detail buttons.

Lastly, get security certificates and trust symbols to increase your relevance and reliability. These will help you reach a higher rank in search engine result pages. Have your website certified by Microsoft, Oracle, and Google. Avail certifications from security systems to guarantee your customers of safety from viruses and malware. This is very important if you will integrate financial transactions through your website. After all, nobody wants to pay using a credit card on a website that is highly suspicious.

There are also accrediting organizations, depending on your industry, that will mark your quality for all the market to see. Even simple bloggers have trust symbols, so better get some, too.

Build your online marketing strategy around a keyword

TV and radio commercials use catchphrases to secure their slots in the memories of audiences and, nowadays, to be adapted by social media and go viral. The same goes for online marketing. It is important for you to find your own catchphrase in the form of a keyword that people can look up on the internet when needing your services.

The relevance of keywords varies from time to time, depending on trends, so you also have to update your keywords and key phrases consistently. However, you should have one main keyword that will represent your whole business, whole website, and whole content so that your SEO efforts will be consistent from the time you start updating your site until search engines truly pick it up for ranking.

For instance, if you were going to sell personalized candles in Memphis, some of the keywords for your contents would be *Memphis candle, candle in Memphis, personalized candles, personalized candles in Memphis,* and *personalized candle seller in Memphis.* However, for your ranking to be more successful, you have to choose one main keyword that will also be constantly present in your business name, tagline, headlines, domain name (if possible), and contents.

You can use keyword research tools and analytics to determine the most searched and most applicable keywords and long-tail keywords for your business and contents. These online tools can provide keyword relevance on a daily basis so you can update your contents accordingly. They can provide accurate reports on the trends, online traffic flow, and guest lists so you can target a specific market more accurately.

There are online tools designed to help you penetrate specific communities and also SEO companies that work to target localities to maximize relevance to a market. Some are free while some have premiums.

Maintain daily presence

Page ranks change more often than you change your clothes. Being able to keep your current rank is not guaranteed because competitors that use the same keywords update their contents and social media posts and signals on a daily basis. What you need to do to continually attract visitors to your site is to post new content and update your followers on your social media accounts every day. Blogging will help you build a network of prospective customers.

If your online business is offering contents, such as in the case of blogging and being an Amazon affiliate, you cannot fail to update because visitors can only go back to your past contents twice.

Interact in sites with high traffic

The whole world wide web is an infinite community of netizens with their own networks that you can penetrate only if you know how to interact with them in the right places at the right times. You have already learned that forums and social media sites are great venues to interact with potential customers, but you can still be smarter by taking advantage of other bloggers' and websites' popularity and high traffic.

Many bloggers team up with other bloggers to "lend" their followers to one another without the visitors knowing it. Many blogsites encourage guest blogging to establish credible backlinks without using anomalous link dropping methods. At the same time, a blog that has guest bloggers produces additional content and generates new followers, similar to how the guest blogger benefits from the ex-deal.

Aside from going active with your own website, you should also be an active participant in other websites, offering your own services and giving consultations for free. You might even be a moderator for some websites, as those with large memberships are often open to administration volunteers. Actively commenting on more popular blogsites is also a great way to advocate and "PR" your expertise. If a webmaster notices you, he might even make you a regular contributor.

What you have to do is to check out niche blogs and informative websites that are close to your field or type of business, and start participating in discussions. You can go as far as offering your own contribution for free, and in return, you will have a complete profile box with a backlink to your home page that readers can easily access. It is best if you can find websites that offer free consultation because that will establish your reputation as an expert in a certain field.

Stick to your business

Home business websites rarely encounter problems with this because they know what they offer and what their businesses are all about. However, for bloggers who make a living from advertisements, affiliate programs, and paid reviews, overlooking this is sometimes inevitable.

In a competition where the most updated and content-filled website wins, it is hard to keep on track on your content without veering a little from your niche. It happened with a lot of review sites that have already expanded into other products and services to gain a larger market. However, what became a success for them may not be a good idea at the slightest for you.

Do not get overwhelmed with huge traffic volume and customer feedback. At the end of the day, the main goal of your business website is still to generate sales and not visitors alone. You have to aim for high conversion (from a reader to a customer) and not simply for plenty of hits.

Integrate affiliate marketing into your marketing strategy

To expand your network of customers, you would surely want to utilize word-of-mouth, and the best way to do that is by integrating affiliate marketing into your system. Referral plays an important role in expanding the network of startup businesses because the recommendation of an ordinary person is more credible to people within the same network than the recommendation of a business (like a business-affiliated blogsite) that might have an ulterior motive (which is to convince readers and convert them into paying customers).

For an even more enticing affiliate program, you can offer freebies and discounts to your followers who will successfully refer paying customers who will close a sale. Giving free electronic gift certificates is now also a popular strategy for online stores as regular customers get more motivation for referring new customers.

If your target market is your own area, affiliate marketing might be more successful as the ties are tighter among residences.

Register with PPC programs

PPC (pay-per-click) advertisements are distributed across various websites by ad vendors that allow your ads to be shown on other websites for better exposure. For just a minimal fee, you can be exposed to millions of netizens worldwide and only with additional payment for successful clicks, registrations, and sales.

With a PPC program, you have the choice to display a banner ad, text ad, or interactive ad. Aside from the successful clicks (thus, the name), the contract price of the ad also depends on the duration of display and size of advertisement. If you decide to handpick the websites where your ads will be displayed, you also have to pay an extra premium, but at least, you will get to choose the best venues for your ads to work.

Lastly, remember that advertisements do not guarantee successful sales but guarantee exposure that might get you potential customers.

Generate your own marketing leads

By adding a *register* button where visitors can key in their email addresses or telephone numbers for free newsletters, digital catalogues, and updates like discount promos and new offers, you can gather a lot of marketing leads that are also your potential customers. You can steadily expand that list from which you will get your priority customers for higher chances of closing a deal.

Adding *like* and *add* buttons to your home page will also make it easier for your visitors to share your contents, sales pages, and online catalogues to their friends and contacts in their social media accounts. You should also know that social media signals and positive feedback, such as "likes," now add to your relevance as perceived by search engines. Higher relevance is equivalent to higher SERP ranking.

Chapter 3: The Beauty and the Advantages of Money Making Online Strategies

Have you noticed that money in your life seems to move with certain dynamics, acting as if it is driving in a one-way street, out of your pocket, and straight into the pockets of others?

Well, if you say yes, then it is time to lure the money straight back into your pocket. I am really uninterested in teaching you how to spend your money – my only interest is to teach you how to thicken your wallet without thinning out your nerves!

How do you know if you are qualified to join the serious online money making exclusive club?

If you are a living, breathing human being who has basic computer skills, then you are more than qualified. As a matter of fact, just by knowing that you read this, I proclaim you as qualified.

Every person needs to have basic working equipment, and in this case, you need a working computer with internet access and a regular mobile phone with a built-in camera or a point and shoot camera.

Usually, when you start your own business, you are required to have an initial investment.

In this case, you need nothing, zero dollars!

What you need is a desire to work and have fun while doing it so you can load up your PayPal account or your wallet, in case you prefer cash!

You can read all about these three online money making options, study them, and try your luck in one or all of them simultaneously, which I advise wholeheartedly!

Your check loaded up with money from your online money making platforms is within reach; what you need to do is reach out and grab it!

Chapter 4: What It Takes to Get the Job Done

In order for you to embark on the idea of starting your own part-time home-based business, which will one day blossom into a full-time income and allow you to quit the rat race, you need to start with the right mindset. The mindset that I am referring to is this: you need a full-time mindset for this part-time business. In other words, you cannot be working a part-time business thinking, "Well, I don't have to give it my all, because after all, it is a part-time business," or "I can do this while watching my favorite show because after all, I am only doing this part time, and if it catches on, then great." Do you see where I am going with this?

When you are working on this part-time business, you need to think and act like it is the be all and end all – that it will be your main business one day. If that is truly going to happen, you need to treat it with sincerity and with your full cooperation and attention. You have to develop a certain momentum and speed if all your actions are going to add up to something that you can be proud of.

You will learn to leverage your time, your money, your skills, and everything else that is necessary to eventually quit the rat race and live life on your own terms. Just imagine what life would be like when you get to this point. You get up in the morning and guess what... you can work OR you don't have to. You can do some chores OR you don't have to. You can play with the kids OR you can play with the dog. You can go shopping OR you can go to the beach. OR... you can do it all because now, you are living life on your own terms. I hope you "get it" by now.

The best "thing" about your new business is that the income keeps coming in even if you don't show up for work. Try imagining that scenario with your current J.O.B. How long do you think the income would keep on coming in if you decided not to show up for work? I thought so!

So what exactly is it going to take to get you from point A, where you are today as a card-carrying member of the rat race, to point B, where you can tell your boss goodbye and tear up that card in front of all your co-workers?

You are going to have to learn a few new skills. Now mind you, these are not hard to learn, and in fact, many people overcomplicate them, which is totally unnecessary. I will show you the exact skills later on in this book, but just stick with me for now. You will then take these new skills and put them to good use whereby they will get your new online business rolling down the track of success.

This new skill that was just mentioned will become one of the greatest assets that you will learn to help you quit the rat race. Just like some of your current skills that you employ in your current job, this new skill will allow you to leverage your time far beyond your imagination. Along the way, I am going to show you how to monetize these emails so that your subscribers will be more than happy to hand over their hard-earned money to you in exchange for the valuable information that you are going to give them. This information, of course, can take on any one of several forms, such as an ebook just like the one you are reading now, or a membership service, just like the one I mentioned in the preface, or a software download, or even a physical product.

Only your imagination can put a limit on what this information for sale will hold. The only thing that is really important at this point is that the information is valuable, factual, and beneficial for your subscribers, which will make them want to stay "tuned in" to you and your future emails. You will develop a reputation in no time, and the last thing that you want to happen would be to tarnish that reputation by sending out an email that is less than true or undesirable or not in tune with your subscribers.

Chapter 5: The Best Online Business Model for You

In case you might wondering what particular home-based business model you should use for yourself, then these are some of the popular online business models for you.

Blogging

The main reason that blogging is in the number one spot is because many of the other online business models can be performed through blogging. In fact, many successful marketers started out as bloggers until they realized that there is a better monetary model. Now, if you are on a tight budget, it is entirely possible to set up your own online blog for free. Blogger.com comes to mind, but there are others. Take my advice, and don't do it. If you use a free platform, the owner of the platform owns all your hard work, and if they cease to exist, guess what, so do you.

A better alternative to starting your own blog on a free platform is to start by buying your own domain name from any one of several sources; Godaddy and Namecheap come to mind. You would pay about $10.00 or less for it. Try to get a .com or a .net or a .org name extension, as these are highly regarded. As for the name itself, there used to be a lot of emphasis on getting what is called an exact match domain name. So for instance, in the diving scenario alluded to previously, you might try to buy Floridakeysdivingspots.com or .net or .org. or something very similar. If you couldn't get it because it is already taken, you could try adding dashes as in Florida-keys-diving-spots.com. The truth of the matter is that exact match domain names don't carry the weight that they once did, so I wouldn't stress out too much over it. As a matter of fact, since you are not going to be relying on search engine optimization (SEO) too much to get a good ranking in the search engines, the domain name you pick really doesn't matter anymore.

Now that you have purchased your own domain name, you will need to have it hosted for you. That is how your work will show up on the web. It has to be hosted by a web server in order for other people to see it. Again, similar to purchasing a domain name, there are many hosts from which you can choose. Hostgator and Bluehost come to mind. In some cases, you can let the company from which you bought the domain name host it for you as well. At the time of this writing, Godaddy was having a giant sale: 99 cents for a domain name and $3.49 per month for hosting. A quick calculation shows that you can be up and running on the internet for less than $50.00 per year! This is very reasonable; just read the fine print, if any.

Your blog is up and running, so it is time to monetize it or, to put it another way, it is time to extract some money from your visitors. While there are many ways to do this, many of them have a common denominator, and that is you are playing the role of an affiliate. An affiliate is someone who receives a commission in exchange for sending someone (your visitor) to the affiliate site in the hopes of garnering a sale. In some cases, no sale at all has to be made; simply sending a visitor is all that is required in order to receive a commission. The most common version of this is known as Google AdSense.

Affiliate Marketing

Affiliate marketing is you as the affiliate, earning a commission from each sale you facilitate by promoting someone else's product or service. The best feature of affiliate marketing is that you don't need to create your own product or service. Instead, you make money by sending traffic to an advertiser's product or service.

Most affiliate programs require the visitor to perform an action or make a purchase in order for you, as the site owner, to receive a commission. The affiliate program that you join – and by the way, this should be somewhat related to the material on your page and website – will have tools for you to use to market their program. So to use our dive example, you would sign up with XYZ diving tours. A typical tour might cost $100.00. XYZ diving tours will give you a banner to place in a strategic spot on your site so that when the site visitor sees the banner, he or she might click on it because it is advertising some great tour, and lo and behold, XYZ diving tours will pay you a commission of $40.00 (or whatever).

Network Marketing/MLM

We will now move on to network marketing and or multilevel marketing. This type of marketing has gained somewhat of a bad reputation because of so many people who have gotten burned by it. You know the routine. You join company X to push their product, and you are led to believe that the real money is in your downline, so it is in your best interest to recruit as many people as possible into the network. Usually, there is an initiation fee and the prospect of eternal riches if you and your downline buy a boatload of company x's product.

While there may be many variations of this concept, the bottom line is the same.

Whose company do you want to build: your own or that of company X? I think the answer should steer you far away from this type of business model. Even if it is a solid company like Amway or Mary Kay or Avon, the question still stands: Whose company do you want to build: your own or that of company X? I think you are tired of building someone else's company, which is why you bought this book in the first place... right!

Freelance Services

Your skills are very important in deciding on your perfect home job. Maybe you are a good writer or a graphic artist, or maybe you possess any other talent that is needed by website owners to keep functioning day in and day out. If so, you can earn an online income by selling your services outright or by joining a company that needs people with talent like yours. There are three companies that come to mind that could put your services to good use. They are Elance, ODesk, and Fiverr, but before you say "where do I sign," keep in mind that working for them as opposed to pure freelancing is, once again, building up someone else's business.

Article Marketing

Yes, you could write some articles on your chosen passion and have them link back to your blog, but if you go down this road you will become frustrated very quickly as it will not lead to the monetary gains that you seek in order to quit the rat race. You are much better off using your writing talent to write emails that you are going to send out with the business model that we first spoke about. Believe it, commit to it, and take action. The money will follow, and in no time at all, you will be able to quit the rat race.

Miscellaneous Model Job

Finally, we have our miscellaneous section (everything has a miscellaneous section, doesn't it?). Here, we see things like taking surveys, buying and selling domain names, arbitrage offerings, which is simply the buying of any online service at one price and reselling the same service at a higher price, and the list goes on and on, but you must believe me when I tell you that the first business model that we talked about is, by far, the best. Get that down right, and you will never have to worry about where your next meal is coming from!

The Potential with Affiliate Marketing

Affiliate marketing is a business opportunity that, if mastered, can generate a lot of profit, but it should never be taken for granted. It does have the potential to lead anyone to make regrettable decisions, just like in any other profession. It is just like the risks taken in the stock market and forex, where success cannot be always guaranteed.

There is a lot of potential in affiliate marketing if you are willing to invest the time required to be good at it, gather a customer base, and create content that will help sell your products. While it is a time-consuming process, it is also the kind of job that can generate a lot of profits. Despite the obstacles you will face along the way, the ultimate result will be financial independence and a long-term job that will keep you entertained.

You must remember that all good things generally come to those who persevere and show patience, even in the face of adversity and failure. Affiliate marketing is a diverse field with many opportunities, methods, and approaches to consider. If your first plan doesn't work out, you shouldn't shy away from experimentation. Take it one day at a time, and test out different strategies to see what kind of results you can produce.

It's also important to keep in mind that affiliate marketing most likely won't be an overnight realization of all your dreams, so you must be careful not to make rash decisions, such as quitting your day job right away or anything of that nature. You need to make this a smooth transition that is as

Alan Anderson

gradual as it has to be depending on your life's circumstances. If you take it slow, the risks will truly be negligible.

Whether your ambition is to quit a job you hate or soothe your workaholic itch by acquiring additional income in your spare time, creativity and patience are sure to keep you on the right track to success. Once you feel your first affiliate marketing dollars in your hand or deposited into your account, the feeling of success will wash over you in an awesome way. Even if your first payment is negligible, it will be enough to show you the possibilities and keep you going forward. With a bit of focus, you may find yourself living your dream life sooner than expected.

Conclusion

Working at home can be a dream come true or it can be a nightmare. Its success depends upon your willingness to go the extra mile. Working from home does not mean sitting next to the bay window, daydreaming or surfing the net all day. It takes hard work and dedication in order to make money.

When telecommuting as an employee, keep in mind that it is a job perk and a privilege. Your employer is putting trust in your ability to perform without being micromanaged. As a business owner, you are not going to be able to slack off when it comes to rules and regulations. You will be shut down in a heartbeat if you try to avoid permits, licensing, and taxes.

Finally, I'd like to ask you a favor, if I may. If you enjoyed this book, then I'd really appreciate you leaving a review and your feedback on Amazon. You can do that by writing a review in your Amazon account under Your Orders.

Thank you, and good luck!

WOULDN'T IT BE GREAT IF YOU COULD WATCH YOUR OWN MONEY GROW ITSELF TO EXPONENTIAL PROPORTIONS?

Investing is your friend. While the prospect of dabbling into investments may seem difficult for beginners or even those who have some knowledge, the rewards can be amazing. This book will teach you how to begin investing like a pro through detailed strategies and techniques.

Here's what's in store for you:

- Investing basics for those just starting to get their feet wet
- Investing in stocks and options
- Investing in bonds and mutual funds
- Investing in ETFs and precious metals
- Investing in dividend stocks
- Compare different stock markets
- Find a strategy that's right for you
- Maximize your income potential
- And much more!

Visit to Order Your Copy Today!
https://www.amazon.com/dp/1517050863

TODAY IS THE DAY, TAKE CHARGE OF YOUR TEAM!

The idea behind writing this book was to use my experience to help those starting out and to be able to give useful and sound advice. There are many corporate style books on leadership. What makes mine different is that it's written by someone who has been where you are currently standing, and who understands your difficulty with being faced with the job of team leader for the first time. Walk through the pages and learn how it's done. It's actually easier than you may imagine, once you know what it is that you need to be doing.

In this book you will learn how to:

- Effectively communicate with your team
- Allocate and delegate
- Identify your teams strengths and weaknesses
- Develop your coaching skills
- Manage conflict resolution
- Improve your coaching skills
- Become a great leader
- And much, much more

Visit to Order Your Copy Today!
https://www.amazon.com/dp/1518821782